STARTING RIGHT

THE BIBLICAL GUIDE
TO A SUCCESSFUL MARRIAGE

LIVING
FAITH
BOOKS

Director: Brandon Briscoe
Editor: Melissa Wharton
Designer: Joel Springer
Cover Photo: Rian Stallbaumer
Written by: Larry & Anita Smith, Kenny Morgan, and Brandon Briscoe
ISBN: 978-1-950004-07-2
Copyright © 2021 Living Faith Fellowship

Table of Contents

Introduction	7
Lesson 1 / The Purpose for Marriage	11
Lesson 2 / The Roles of Marriage	23
Lesson 3 / Family Finances	35
Lesson 4 / Conflict in Marriage	45
Lesson 5 / Intimacy	57
Lesson 6 / Moving Forward	73

Introduction

Eph 5:22-33 *Wives, submit yourselves unto your own husbands, as unto the Lord. 23 For the husband is the head of the wife, even as Christ is the head of the church: and he is the saviour of the body. 24 Therefore as the church is subject unto Christ, so let the wives be to their own husbands in every thing. 25 Husbands, love your wives, even as Christ also loved the church, and gave himself for it; 26 That he might sanctify and cleanse it with the washing of water by the word, 27 That he might present it to himself a glorious church, not having spot, or wrinkle, or any such thing; but that it should be holy and without blemish. 28 So ought men to love their wives as their own bodies. He that loveth his wife loveth himself. 29 For no man ever yet hated his own flesh; but nourisheth and cherisheth it, even as the Lord the church: 30 For we are members of his body, of his flesh, and of his bones. 31 For this cause shall a man leave his father and mother, and shall be joined unto his wife, and they two shall be one flesh. 32 This is a great mystery: but I speak concerning Christ and the church. 33 Nevertheless let every one of you in particular so love his wife even as himself; and the wife see that she reverence her husband.*

This passage in Ephesians is one of the most incredible in the Bible. It reveals to us that marriage is a picture of the unity of Christ and his bride, the church. The marriage relationship is extremely important to God because through it, man and woman become one flesh and fulfill God's desire to reproduce both physically and spiritually. Also note in this passage the enormous love and unity that God desires in marriage, including the limitless dedication the husband is to give his wife (like Christ toward us) and the reverence the wife is to give her husband (like the church toward Christ).

Premarital or marital counseling is being provided to you in order to help you be a couple that brings glory to the Lord. Through these lessons, you will gain an understanding of why God created marriage, what he wants to accomplish through it, and what each of your responsibilities will be in marriage. It will also prompt you to discuss and work out differences in thinking in order to help you reduce conflict throughout your marriage.

This is not about completing a series of lessons, but about learning who God wants you to be as a married couple with a life dedicated to him. Learning is always easier when it's modeled. You are encouraged to intentionally observe and communicate with your counselors to learn how they relate to each other on a daily basis and function in life and ministry together. Let's consider some guidelines for your time together.

The Responsibilities of the Couple:

1. Be faithful in attendance

    Remember that your counselors are donating their time to help you, so be respectful and dedicated.

2. Be accountable to assignments

    Each assignment is designed to prepare you for success in marriage.

3. Be completely transparent and honest

   Your counselors can help you work through possible areas of problem or conflict. It is helpful to resolve these now, so they don't hurt your relationship after you're married.

4. Be blameless and don't sin

   Be careful not to put yourself in compromising situations that put you at risk for sexual sin. **Pro 6:27; 1Co 6:18**

The Responsibilities of Your Counselors:

1. They will be prepared to teach you biblical principles of marriage.

2. They will be to spend time with you to discuss and address questions beyond the lessons.

3. They will be discreet

   Your counselors seek to maintain confidentiality. Only in rare cases would it be important to share information up the chain (with a pastor, for instance) if additional information or expertise is needed to help you.

4. They will be available to you long-term to be advisors in the months and years after your marriage. It is very helpful for a newly married couple to have ongoing mentorship in marriage as you encounter the various challenges and seasons of marriage.

Lesson 1

The Purpose of Marriage

It's important to understand God's intention in designing the institution of marriage. The more a married couple understands his purposes, the better equipped they are to understand what a successful marriage is and aim for it.

The key word of this lesson:

RELATIONSHIP

The key questions this lesson answers:

What is God's definition of marriage?

What are God's goals for marriage?

The key purpose of this lesson:

The purpose of this lesson is to explain why God created marriage and how the husband and wife fit into His plan.

The key point of this lesson:

God created marriage in order that we achieve His goal of being fruitful and multiplying, both physically and spiritually.

The key verses:

Gen 2:18 And the LORD God said, It is not good that the man should be alone; I will make him an help meet for him.

Gen 1:28 And God blessed them, and God said unto them, Be fruitful, and multiply, and replenish the earth,

Discussion Question: Before we begin, share about the example of marriage that you grew up with. What were some of the good and bad things you learned from watching your parents' relationship?

I. The Definition of Marriage

Marriage is the God-designed union between one man and one woman in relationship with Him.

Gen 2:18-25 And the LORD God said, It is not good that the man should be alone; I will make him an help meet for him. 19 And out of the ground the LORD God formed every beast of the field, and every fowl of the air; and brought them unto Adam to see what he would call them: and whatsoever Adam called every living creature, that was the name thereof. 20 And Adam gave names to all cattle, and to the fowl of the air, and to every beast of the field; but for Adam there was not found an help meet for him. 21 And the LORD God caused a deep sleep to fall upon Adam, and he slept: and he took one of his ribs, and closed up the flesh instead thereof; 22 And the rib, which the LORD God had taken from man, made he a woman, and brought her unto the man. 23 And Adam said, This is now bone of my bones, and flesh of my flesh: she shall be called Woman, because she was taken out of Man. 24 Therefore shall a man leave his father and his mother, and shall cleave unto his wife: and they shall be one flesh. 25 And they were both naked, the man and his wife, and were not ashamed.

Definition #1: The institution of marriage originated with God, not man. Therefore, God is the ultimate expert and authority on marriage, not man.

And the LORD God said,...

Definition #2: The institution of marriage was created by God to address man's need for companionship.

...It is not good that the man should be alone; I will make him an help meet for him.

Definition #3: The institution of marriage joins together the husband and wife as one.

And Adam said, This is now bone of my bones, and flesh of my flesh...

Definition #4: The biblical institution of marriage excludes polygamy and homosexuality.

- Polygamy undermines the holy union between one man and one woman.

Exo 20:14 *Thou shalt not commit adultery.*

- Homosexuality undermines the physical design between one man and one woman.

Rom 1:26 *For this cause God gave them up unto vile affections: for even their women did change the natural use into that which is against nature:*

Definition #5: The institution of marriage is intended to be a lifelong commitment.

Mat 19:4 And he answered and said unto them, Have ye not read, that he which made [them] at the beginning made them male and female, 5 And said, For this cause shall a man leave father and mother, and shall cleave to his wife: and they twain shall be one flesh? 6 Wherefore they are no more twain, but one flesh. What therefore God hath joined together, let not man put asunder.

II. The Purpose of Marriage

To describe the purpose of marriage, it's important to understand why God created marriage.

Purpose #1: Worship

We worship when our life ascribes value and honor to God in a way that pleases him.

- **We worship God first as individuals**

This means that the predominant identity of a married person is not first-and-foremost to be a good husband or wife, but a true worshipper. A Christian home should reflect a couple's mutual desire to worship God with every aspect of their lives.

Joh 4:23 But the hour cometh, and now is, when the true worshippers shall worship the Father in spirit and in truth: for the Father seeketh such to worship him. 24 God [is] a Spirit: and they that worship him must worship [him] in spirit and in truth.

  o **In spirit** – to worship God in sincerity of heart and mind

  o **In truth** – to worship God in accordance to his word

- **We worship God vocally**

This means that a couple should commit to collectively speak and sing God's praises.

Psa 71:8 *Let my mouth be filled with thy praise and with thy honour all the day.*

- **We worship God by fulfilling our God-given spousal roles.**

This means that couples should know and live according to the distinct responsibilities God gives a husband and wife.

In Colossians 3:17, God describes a lifestyle of worship that includes the things we say and the things we do. Then, in verses 18 and 19, he further describes how we live this way in the context of marriage by fulfilling our distinct responsibilities.

Col 3:17 *And whatsoever ye do in word or deed, [do] all in the name of the Lord Jesus, giving thanks to God and the Father by him. 18 Wives, submit yourselves unto your own husbands, as it is fit in the Lord. 19 Husbands, love [your] wives, and be not bitter against them... 23 And whatsoever ye do, do it heartily, as to the Lord, and not unto men;*

- **We worship God by surrendering to Him**

This means we turn over control of our personal aspirations, opinions, and resources to God, knowing that he is a good father with good plans for our lives.

Rom 12:1 *I beseech you therefore, brethren, by the mercies of God, that ye present your bodies a living sacrifice, holy, acceptable unto God, which is your reasonable service.*

> **Discussion Question: What would marriage look like if we refused to worship rightly?**

Purpose #2: Fellowship

We fellowship as we commune with God and others in the body of Christ.

- **We should first have fellowship with God**

This means we pursue him by reading and studying the Bible as well as seeking him in prayer. This establishes us in a healthy relationship of love and communication.

Deu 4:29 *But if from thence thou shalt seek the LORD thy God, thou shalt find [him], if thou seek him with all thy heart and with all thy soul.*

In God's original plan, man was to have eternal fellowship with Him. Therefore, fellowship with God is a clear goal of marriage.

- **We should have fellowship one with another**

The byproduct of our fellowship with God will be fellowship within the marriage relationship, just as with the body of Christ as a whole.

1Jo 1: 5 *This then is the message which we have heard of him, and declare unto you, that God is light, and in him is no darkness at all. 6 If we say that we have fellowship with him, and walk in darkness, we lie, and do not the truth: 7 But if we walk in the light, as he is in the light, we have fellowship one with another, and the blood of Jesus Christ his Son cleanseth us from all sin.*

Acts 18:1-4 *In scripture, we find a married couple named Acquilla and Priscilla. This couple is always mentioned together; they were inseparable. What fueled their close fellowship in marriage was their shared fellowship with God and their desire to serve him.*

Purpose #3: Fruitfulness

We are called to be fruitful as we multiply and establish God's purposes within the earth.

- **We can be fruitful physically.**

God has given man the ability to reproduce so that we might fill the earth with offspring and raise them to follow God.

Gen 1:28 *And God blessed them, and God said unto them, Be fruitful, and multiply, and replenish the earth, and subdue it: and have dominion over the fish of the sea, and over the fowl of the air, and over every living thing that moveth upon the earth.*

- Children are a blessing from the Lord to the family

Psa 127:3-5 *Lo, children are an heritage of the LORD: and the fruit of the womb is his reward. 4 As arrows are in the hand of a mighty man; so are children of the youth. 5 Happy is the man that hath his quiver full of them: they shall not be ashamed, but they shall speak with the enemies in the gate.*

- Most married couples desire to have children physically. However, in some cases, infertility issues arise. In such cases, couples should take comfort in the following truths:

1. God is still good

Psa 34:8 *O taste and see that the LORD is good: blessed is the man that trusteth in him.*

2. God is righteous in all his ways

Psa 145:17 *The LORD [is] righteous in all his ways, and holy in all his works.*

3. God loves all His children equally

Rom 8:38 *For I am persuaded, that neither death, nor life, nor angels, nor principalities, nor powers, nor things present, nor things to come, 39 Nor height, nor depth, nor any other creature, shall be able to separate us from the love of God, which is in Christ Jesus our Lord.*

4. God's grace is sufficient

2Co 12:9 *And he said unto me, My grace is sufficient for thee: for my strength is made perfect in weakness. Most gladly therefore will I rather glory in my infirmities, that the power of Christ may rest upon me.*

5. The marriage still has a purpose

Eph 2:10 *For we are his workmanship, created in Christ Jesus unto good works, which God hath before ordained that we should walk in them.*

6. Contentment is attainable

Php 4:11 *Not that I speak in respect of want: for I have learned, in whatsoever state I am, therewith to be content. 12 I know both how to be abased, and I know how to abound: every where and in all things I am instructed both to be full and to be hungry, both to abound and to suffer need.*

- **We can be fruitful spiritually**

God has given the believer the ability to reproduce his worship and fill his kingdom with disciples. **Jhn 15:8**

The Great Commission is the New Testament's call to be spiritually fruitful.

***Mat 28:18** And Jesus came and spake unto them, saying, All power is given unto me in heaven and in earth. 19 Go ye therefore, and teach all nations, baptizing them in the name of the Father, and of the Son, and of the Holy Ghost: 20 Teaching them to observe all things whatsoever I have commanded you: and, lo, I am with you alway, even unto the end of the world. Amen.*

For the Apostle Paul, those he brought up in the faith as spiritual sons gave him immense joy.

***1Ti 1:2** Unto Timothy, [my] own son in the faith: Grace, mercy, [and] peace, from God our Father and Jesus Christ our Lord.*

Spiritual fruitfulness for the married couple is more important than physical fruitfulness, so go and make disciples of Jesus!

Purpose #4: Faithfulness

- **We should be faithful to God**

This means that our worship should be exclusive.

The first of the Ten Commandments given to Israel speaks to what was of extreme importance to God as it concerned their relationship with him:

***Exodus 20:3** Thou shalt have no other gods before me.*

Anything that gets in the way of worshipping God (e.g. people, places, things, ideas, desires) is an act of spiritual adultery.

- **We should be faithful to one another**

This means that the marriage relationship is exclusive intellectually, emotionally, spiritually and physically.

This means that we must refuse to entertain impulses or thoughts of leaving or divorcing our spouse.

Exo 20:14 Thou shalt not commit adultery.

Mar 10:5 And Jesus answered and said unto them, For the hardness of your heart he wrote you this precept. 6 But from the beginning of the creation God made them male and female. 7 For this cause shall a man leave his father and mother, and cleave to his wife; 8 And they twain shall be one flesh: so then they are no more twain, but one flesh. 9 What therefore God hath joined together, let not man put asunder.

This also means that we must refuse to entertain ourselves with imagery that tempts us in any way to be unfaithful. Being unfaithful in one's thought life is just as sinful to God as being unfaithful in action. This includes interacting with pornography, erotic novels, and filthy movies. Pornography is a huge plague in the church today, and Satan often uses it to destroy marriages

Mat 5:28 But I say unto you, That whosoever looketh on a woman to lust after her hath committed adultery with her already in his heart.

Eph 5:3 But fornication, and all uncleanness, or covetousness, let it not be once named among you,

If the areas of pornography and lust are a struggle for you, consider meeting with your counselor (male with male, female with female) to discuss what it means to overcome these struggles.

Homework

In a wedding, a bride and groom are asked to recite vows. These vows should reflect a desire to obey God and commit oneself to their spouse. Often the vows are variations on the following:

"GROOM, do you take this woman to be your lawful, wedded wife? In the presence of God and these witnesses, do you promise to love her, comfort her, honor and keep her, in sickness and in health, in prosperity and adversity, and forsaking all others, to be to her in all things a true and faithful husband, as long as you both shall live?

BRIDE, do you take this man to be your lawful, wedded husband? In the presence of God and these witnesses, do you promise to love him, comfort him, honor and keep him, in sickness and in health, in prosperity and adversity, and forsaking all others, to be to him in all things a true and faithful wife, as long as you both shall live?"

After studying this lesson, what are some other biblical vows a couple could make? Whether you choose to recite them in your actual wedding or not, write out some vows and bring those next time to share.

Lesson 2

The Roles of Marriage

It's important to understand the roles and responsibilities the Lord assigns to the husband and to the wife in marriage. If each of you commits to fulfilling these roles in a biblical way, you are very likely to have a successful marriage.

The key words of this lesson for women are:

SUBMIT & RESPECT

The key words of this lesson for men are:

LOVE & LEAD

The key question this lesson answers:

What are the roles of the wife in a biblical marriage?

What are the roles of the husband in a biblical marriage?

The key purpose of this lesson:

To understand the role assigned to each couple in marriage.

The key point of this lesson:

Each spouse has distinct roles and responsibilities that they must fulfill in order to glorify God through marriage.

The key verses:

Eph 5:22 Wives, submit yourselves unto your own husbands, as unto the Lord. 23 For the husband is the head of the wife, even as Christ is the head of the church: and he is the saviour of the body. 24 Therefore as the church is subject unto Christ, so [let] the wives [be] to their own husbands in every thing. 25 Husbands, love your wives, even as Christ also loved the church, and gave himself for it; ... 33 Nevertheless let every one of you in particular so love his wife even as himself; and the wife [see] that she reverence [her] husband.

1Pe 3:7 Likewise, ye husbands, dwell with them according to knowledge, giving honour unto the wife, as unto the weaker vessel, and as being heirs together of the grace of life; that your prayers be not hindered.

Introducing the Roles of Marriage

When we describe the roles of marriage, we mean the distinct responsibilities that God has given a husband and a wife.

The Wife's Role #1: Women are responsible for following their husband

Eph 5:22 Wives, submit yourselves unto your own husbands, as unto the Lord.

- **The wife is equal but distinct**

Christian wives and husbands are equal in status before God but do not have the same function/role.

Gal 3: 28 *There is neither Jew nor Greek, there is neither bond nor free, there is neither male nor female: for ye are all one in Christ Jesus.*

- **The wife is called to submit**

In the marriage relationship, just like in the human body, there can only be one head; functionally, the husband is the head. According to Ephesians 5:22, the wife should submit herself to her husband; this means she is willing to follow him as long as he leads biblically.

1Co 11:3 *But I would have you know, that the head of every man is Christ; and the head of the woman [is] the man; and the head of Christ [is] God.*

Sarah, Abraham's wife is a great example of submission:

1Pe 3:6 *Even as Sara obeyed Abraham, calling him lord: whose daughters ye are, as long as ye do well, and are not afraid with any amazement.*

The Christian wife should never make her husband feel he needs to earn her submission and respect.

Here are some clear principles for wives in following their husbands:

- There is protection in submission. **1Co 11:1-5**

- Wives are the weaker vessel and easier to deceive. **1Pe 3:7**

- God works through spiritual authority. **Pro 21:1**
- Following is a choice, not a feeling. **Col 3:18**

There are many challenges to a Christian wife submitting biblically to her husband.

- Pride
- Popular culture and feminist ideals
- Family and friends' influence and opinions
- Husband's imperfections

Working ladies must reconcile submission to their husbands and submission to their employer, which can sometimes be difficult. Additionally, Christian wives with professional careers who are paid to take charge, direct others, and make decisions must learn that despite their professional role, when they are at home, they are responsible to submit to their husband.

Discussion Question for Wife: Do you recognize any of these challenges in your own perceptions of marriage? In the past, what have your views been on the concept of submission? What reservations have you had? How has this lesson brought new clarity?

The Husband's Role #1: Husbands are responsible for leading their wives

Eph 5:23 *For the husband is the head of the wife, even as Christ is the head of the church: and he is the saviour of the body.*

- **The husbands should reflect Christ**

The Christian husband is to be the head of his home the way Christ is the head of the church. Therefore, the Christian husband must reflect Christ in thought, speech, and behavior before his wife.

1Jo 2:6 He that saith he abideth in him ought himself also so to walk, even as he walked.

The Christian husband is responsible to lead his wife. This includes, but is not limited to:

- o Watching over his wife **1Pe 3:7**

- o Setting vision for the home **Pro 29:18**

- o Defining how his wife can help him **Gen 2:18**

- o Prioritizing the Word of God and the local church in the home **Eph 5:26**

- o Establishing the boundaries for parents and family **Gen 2:24**

- o Taking the lead in training and disciplining children **Eph 6:4**

- o Ensure his family is provided for intellectually, emotionally, spiritually, and physically **1Ti 5:8**

- **The husband is accountable**

Every Christian husband must reconcile that he is responsible for his wife and that God will judge him for how he leads her. It is Adam who finds himself accountable before God after "the sin"…

Gen 3:9 *And the LORD God called unto Adam, and said unto him, Where [art] thou? 10 And he said, I heard thy voice in the garden, and I was afraid, because I [was] naked; and I hid myself. 11 And he said, Who told thee that thou [wast] naked? Hast thou eaten of the tree, whereof I commanded thee that thou shouldest not eat?*

> **Discussion Question for Husband: Describe how Jesus Christ led in his earthly ministry and is leading his church today. Do you have men of God in your life who set a leadership example in marriage and ministry? Share some practical ways in which you see them lead.**

The Wife's Role #2: Women are responsible for ministering to their husband

Eph 5:22 *Wives, submit yourselves unto your own husbands, as unto the Lord.*

- **The wife ministers to her husband by having high character**

A wife should have high integrity so that her husband can put his heart and trust in her hands.

Pro 31:11 *The heart of her husband doth safely trust in her, so that he shall have no need of spoil.*

- **The wife ministers to her husband by supporting him**

A wife is called to support her husband emotionally, physically, intellectually, and spiritually from day to day as her husband leads their home and in ministry.

Php 2:3 *[Let] nothing [be done] through strife or vainglory; but* *in lowliness of mind let each esteem other better than themselves. 4 Look not every man on his own things, but every man also on the things of others.*

Pro 31:12 *She will do him good and not evil all the days of her life.*

- **The wife ministers to her husband by being wise and kind**

A wife should walk in the Spirit so that her speech and actions are in accordance to God's will and the leadership of her husband. No wife is perfect in this regard, but every Christian wife should strive to this end.

Pro 31:26 *She openeth her mouth with wisdom; and in her tongue [is] the law of kindness.*

When learning to minister to your husband, there are some practical things to consider:

- Never forget you are subject to your husband. **Eph 5:22**

- Never undermine the direction God has given your husband. **Gen 25:28; 27:8-11**

- Never entertain critical thoughts against your husband. **1Co 13:5**

- Never speak evil about your husband (which may be particularly tempting around relatives or friends). **Php 2:14**

- If you are having a problem in your marriage relationship, handle it biblically. **Mat 18:15-17**

- Never compare your husband against other men. **2Co 10:12**

- Never share intimate thoughts or emotions with any other men. There is a danger in allowing your posture and dialogue with other men to be "too comfortable". **Pro 7:19-22; Jas 3:5**

- Never use sexual intimacy as either a reward or punishment. **1Co 7:14**

- Never make decisions that impact the marriage without consulting your husband. **Ecc 4:9**

Discussion Question for Wife: In what areas of life and ministry do you know that you can begin supporting your husband, even right now?

<u>The Husband's Role #2: Husbands are responsible for loving their wife</u>

Eph 5:25 Husbands, love your wives, even as Christ also loved the church, and gave himself for it;

- **Husbands should love their wives sacrificially**

When we look at Christ, we discover what it means to love sacrificially. Sacrifice means it will cost you something to ensure that your wife is held in higher importance than your own desires and purposes. This impacts the way you conduct yourself at home, the way you provide financial security, the way you minister, and the way you spend your time.

Are you willing to be sacrificial in love and devotion to your bride?

Consider Christ's sacrifice...

- Christ gave up his heavenly position where he was reverenced as Lord of lords

- He came down and lived for 33 years on a sinful earth
- He submitted to the authority of human parents and government
- He lived the life of a traveling prophet with no residence or wealth
- He spent His ministry giving himself for the good of others
- He endured ongoing persecution by His created beings
- He was falsely accused, tried, and convicted of a crime by his own creation
- He was beaten beyond recognition
- He was crucified — the most humiliating and torturous method of execution
- He died, was buried, and rose again for the salvation of mankind

It's easy to make vows on a wedding day, but are you truly willing to live this way every day, every way, no excuses and no days off? In the power of Christ, it's possible.

- **Husbands should love their wife unconditionally**

When we look at Christ, we also discover what it means to love unconditionally. Unconditional love is not dependent on anything your wife does or does not do for you. Whether or not she meets your expectations plays no part in obeying God by loving her. **A wife should never feel as though she must earn this kind of love.** After all, none of us did anything to earn Christ's love. **Rom 11:6; Eph 2:8-9**

- **Husbands should love their wife in a diversity of ways**

A husband's love towards his wife should reflect all the types of love we see in scripture. These three Greek words in the Bible capture those types of love.

- *Agape* (Greek)

This is the type of love that Christ has for the church; it's sacrificial, unconditional, and compassionate. It's the type of love that prefers your spouse over yourself. **Jhn 3:16**

- *Phileo* (Greek)

This is the type of love between a brother and sister in Christ. This love establishes lines of communication, empathy, comradery, and shared vision. **Heb 13:1**

- *Ahabah* (Hebrew)

Often identified as *eros* in Greek. This is the type of love that is romantic, affectionate, and sexual. This kind of love provokes a desire for physical intimacy and emotive expressions. **Pro 5:18-19**

Discussion Question for Husband: Why is the phrase "fallen out of love" an unbiblical one?

Homework

Take some time this week as an individual and make a list describing habits, relationships, or personal interests that have the potential to interfere with the role God has given you as a spouse. If you recognize that there is a need to discuss these issues, submit your individual lists to your counselors at your next meeting. If you so choose, your counselor will review it with you privately to discuss how to get victory in these areas and pray with you.

Lesson 3

Family Finances

We know that the world's way of managing finances is often in direct opposition to what God instructs, and that financial disagreements are a leading cause of divorce in America. The purpose of this lesson is to teach God's way of managing family finances.

The key word of this lesson:

STEWARDSHIP

The key question this lesson answers:

What is the correct way to manage finances?

The key purpose of this lesson:

To give the Bible's clear and definite teaching on family finances.

The key point of this lesson:

God's way of managing finances is not always easy, but it is always best. Obedience is critical to financial blessing for the Christian couple.

The key verses:

Luk 16:11 *If therefore ye have not been faithful in the unrighteous mammon, who will commit to your trust the true riches?*

Pro 21:20 *There is treasure to be desired and oil in the dwelling of the wise; but a foolish man spendeth it up.*

I. Principles for Financial Stewardship

The Bible provides precepts to guide us in how to handle money and economic resources.

Stewardship Principle #1: Financial stewardship reveals the believer's true heart

Luk 16:11 *If therefore ye have not been faithful in the unrighteous mammon, who will commit to your trust the true riches?*

All the physical resources that God has given us are intended to further his eternal kingdom; how we use our money and financial assets makes a difference eternally. If we mishandle these physical resources on temporary pleasures or poor decision-making, there is a potential we could waste God's spiritual plan for our lives.

Having a good job and making money is not wrong or evil. It's important to note, however, that while God doesn't despise wealth, he does hate greed, pride, covetousness and envy.

1Ti 6:10 *For the* **love of money** *is the root of all evil: which while some coveted after, they have erred from the faith, and pierced themselves through with many sorrows.*

Col 3:2 *Set your affection on things above, not on things on the earth.*

Will you manage your money, or will money manage you?

Stewardship Principle #2: Financial stewardship means working to provide for your family

1Ti 5:8 But if any provide not for his own, and specially for those of his own house, he hath denied the faith, and is worse than an infidel.

God asks that we work to provide for our families. Outside of extenuating factors, every house should have a husband who is working to provide for his family. In some cases, a husband and wife might both work to provide. Regardless of the circumstance, God makes it clear: if we refuse to go out and earn a wage, then we are functioning as a lost person and tempt his chastisement.

Stewardship Principle #3: God promises to meet the needs of obedient stewards

Mat 6:26-33 Behold the fowls of the air: for they sow not, neither do they reap, nor gather into barns; yet your heavenly Father feedeth them. Are ye not much better than they? Which of you by taking thought can add one cubit unto his stature? And why take ye thought for raiment? Consider the lilies of the field, how they grow; they toil not, neither do they spin: And yet I say unto you, That even Solomon in all his glory was not arrayed like one of these. Wherefore, if God so clothe the grass of the field, which to day is, and to morrow is cast into the oven, shall he not much more clothe you, O ye of little faith? Therefore take no thought, saying, What shall we eat? or, What shall we drink? or, Wherewithal shall we be clothed? (For after all these things do the Gentiles seek:) for your heavenly Father knoweth that ye have need of all these things. But seek ye first the kingdom of God, and his righteousness; and all these things shall be added unto you.

While God promises that all those who obey and serve him will have their physical needs met, he doesn't promise they will get all their wants or desires. In other words, God has not promised that Christians deserve (or can produce by means of faith) greater financial success. God knows that all we need to have a secure, rewarding, and successful life is him

Stewardship Principle #4: Financial stewardship means avoiding get rich quick schemes

Pro 28:22 He that hasteth to be rich hath an evil eye, and considereth not that poverty shall come upon him.

Pro 23:4-5 Labour not to be rich: cease from thine own wisdom. Wilt thou set thine eyes upon that which is not? for riches certainly make themselves wings; they fly away as an eagle toward heaven.

The world is full of schemes that promise easy ways to make money or quick fixes for financial dilemmas; beware these forms of entrapment. Examples include gambling and multi-level marketing or investments that are "too good to be true". If you have questions about a financial opportunity, seek counsel from Bible believers in your church who have a testimony of financial wisdom.

II. Principles for Budgeting

When we describe budgeting principles, we mean developing a biblical structure for spending and saving.

Budgeting Principle #1: Budgeting is essential because it promotes financial stability

Pro 21:20 There is treasure to be desired and oil in the dwelling of the wise; but a foolish man spendeth it up.

If you do not have a budget and are just letting your financial situation unfold inconsistently from day to day, then you are allowing your emotions, happenstance, and other people to determine your financial outcomes. A budget helps envision the daily use of your money and support the future intentions of your financial resources.

Pro 29:18 Where there is no vision, the people perish: but he that keepeth the law, happy is he

Budgeting Principle #2: Distinguishing between wants and needs is essential in financial stewardship

A budget will hold you accountable, but it's up to you to first be honest about what you truly need to survive. Making those determinations helps you to prioritize spending and saving over unnecessary, inordinate, and impulsive purchases. Failure to understand wants versus needs will inevitably lead to excessive spending and poor financial management.

Budgeting Principle #3: Honoring the principles of tithing and giving should be essential to every budget

Pro 3:9 Honour the LORD with thy substance, and with the firstfruits of all thine increase:

Disciples of Jesus Christ understand that tithing and giving to the local church supports the work of the ministry and the mission worldwide. If this is not a priority in your home, then it ultimately reflects whether or not God and his purposes are first in every aspect of your life.

Are you tithing? What things do you spend your resources on that could be labeled as wants?

III. Principles for Addressing Debt

It's important to create a plan to stamp out current debts and avoid future debt.

Debt Principle #1: Debt puts you under the control of other people

Pro 22:7 *The rich ruleth over the poor, and the borrower is servant to the lender.*

God is very clear on this matter: if we find ourselves with inordinate debt, then we willingly place ourselves under the control of people and institutions. The outcome is that instead of giving God our servitude, we often find ourselves under the bondage of others.

Debt Principle #2: Consumer debt is often the result of wanting things we do not need

Php 4:11 *Not that I speak in respect of want: for I have learned, in whatsoever state I am, [therewith] to be content.*

This passage reminds us that the Apostle Paul had a mindset and lifestyle based on contentment. He didn't need or want anything that God wasn't willing to provide. He wasn't tempted by the wealth or entertainment of those around him; he was satisfied with exactly what God had provided him in every circumstance or season of life. This is completely different from the materialism and consumerism of our modern world, in that everyone seems to long for the newest fashion, technology, and entertainment. Covetousness is a dangerous sin that has an unending appetite.

Consumer debt could be credit card debt, high car payments, unaffordable mortgages, quick cash loans, foolish investments, premature liquidation of assets, or frivolous and unreasonable academic pursuits.

Debt Principle #3: You can be financially free

2Ti 2:4 No man that warreth entangleth himself with the affairs of [this] life; that he may please him who hath chosen him to be a soldier.

The goal is to be financially unentangled from the world. If you currently have debt, then designing a budget that addresses your debt will help you take practical steps towards this goal. Tackling one debt at a time is a practical way to begin unraveling yourself from the world.

What is your plan to prepare for a life that is financially free?

IV. Principles for Saving & Investing

It's necessary to budget in a way that allows you to prepare for financial trials or future needs.

Saving & Investment Principle #1: Diligent work should produce savings

Pro 21:5 The thoughts of the diligent [tend] only to plenteousness; but of every one [that is] hasty only to want.

If you have full-time employment and manage or reduce your debt, it is healthy for one to begin saving. Savings protect us from financial burden in times of difficulty but also position us to make financial investments.

Saving & Investment Principle #2: You should save enough for unexpected emergencies (e.g. home, auto, health)

Pro 6:6 *Go to the ant, thou sluggard; consider her ways, and be wise: 7 Which having no guide, overseer, or ruler, 8 Provideth her meat in the summer, [and] gathereth her food in the harvest. 9 How long wilt thou sleep, O sluggard? when wilt thou arise out of thy sleep? 10 [Yet] a little sleep, a little slumber, a little folding of the hands to sleep:*

It's impossible to know what tomorrow may bring, and God tells us that it is wise to put away our resources to provide ourselves with some protection against difficult and strenuous times.

Saving & Investment Principle #3: Aggressively pursue paying off debt

Rom 13:8 *Owe no man any thing, but to love one another: for he that loveth another hath fulfilled the law.*

Debt puts us in the bondage of other people but also hinders us from saving and investing.

Saving & Investment Principle #4: Consider a financial plan to ensure inheritance for your family

Pro 13:22 *A good [man] leaveth an inheritance to his children's children: and the wealth of the sinner [is] laid up for the just.*

A budget provides you with a framework to provide for your family, pay off debt, tithe, save, and eventually make investments. A budget makes up the rules that you and your spouse set as a team to help build financial flexibility and freedom as time passes.

Saving & Investment Principle #5: Don't procrastinate investment

Mat 25:26 *His lord answered and said unto him, [Thou] wicked and slothful servant, thou knewest that I reap where I sowed* *not, and gather where I have not strawed: 27 Thou oughtest therefore to have put my money to the exchangers, and [then] at my coming I should have received mine own with usury.*

It's easy to put off the need to invest, particularly when we are surrounded with financial burden. Physical investment, just like spiritual investment, is something you want to prioritize.

Saving & Investment Principle #6: Don't save with proud intentions

Luk 12:16 And he spake a parable unto them, saying, The ground of a certain rich man brought forth plentifully: 17 And he thought within himself, saying, What shall I do, because I have no room where to bestow my fruits? 18 And he said, This will I do: I will pull down my barns, and build greater; and there will I bestow all my fruits and my goods. 19 And I will say to my soul, Soul, thou hast much goods laid up for many years; take thine ease, e at, drink, [and] be merry. 20 But God said unto him, [Thou] fool, this night thy soul shall be required of thee: then whose shall those things be, which thou hast provided?

It is worldly to save and invest with the goal of making yourself unnecessarily comfortable and entertained. Beware of envy and the fleshly temptation to transform wants into needs. Christians are not on earth to build our own little kingdom; if we do, it will only lead to disappointment.

Saving & Investment Principle #7: Never forget to build kingdom wealth

1Co. 3:13 Every man's work shall be made manifest: for the day shall declare it, because it shall be revealed by fire; and the fire shall try every man's work of what sort it is. 14 If any man's work abide which he hath built thereupon, he shall receive a reward. 15 If any man's work shall be burned, he shall suffer loss: but he himself shall be saved; yet so as by fire.

The wisest investment we could ever make is to invest the eternal Word of God into the eternal souls of men. Ultimately, everything else should serve that objective.

Homework

Fill in the attached budget together as a couple. If you feel like you need help or have questions, feel free to discuss it with your counselors in the next meeting.

BUDGET

monthly income	amount	description
salary		
dividends		
total		

expenses	amount	description
mortgage/rent		
car		
phone		
utilities		
healthy insurance		
food		
entertainment		
total		

	amount	description
income total		
- expense total		
= total left		
savings		
investment		

Lesson 4

Conflict Resolution

Every marriage encounters challenges, both from within and without the marriage. This lesson is designed to teach you how to resolve those times of disagreement or challenge in a way that is biblical.

The key word of this lesson:

RESOLVE

The key questions this lesson answers:

How do I resolve issues that will come up with my spouse?

How do we deal with the conflicts that arise from external sources?

The key purpose of this lesson:

To give you a basic understanding of biblical ways to deal with conflict when it occurs.

The key point of this lesson:

Conflict will occur within your marriage. When it does, it must be dealt with quickly and biblically in order to restore unity.

The key verses:

Eph 4:32 *And be ye kind one to another, tenderhearted, forgiving one another, even as God for Christ's sake hath forgiven you.*

Pro 15:1 *A soft answer turneth away wrath: but grievous words stir up anger.*

I. Perspectives on Conflict

When we describe perspectives on conflict, we mean learning to see disagreements and challenges through a biblical viewpoint.

Perspective #1: Know that the enemy is Satan, not your spouse

Eph 6:12 *For we wrestle not against flesh and blood, but against principalities, against powers, against the rulers of the darkness of this world, against spiritual wickedness in high [places].*

Satan targeted the first marriage because he saw it as a threat to his agenda. **Gen 3:1**

His perception of your marriage is no different. If he can cause you to argue, fight, and divide, then he has succeeded in undermining the authority and glory of God and his purpose.

Every couple should anticipate conflict and be prepared to deal with it in love when it happens.

Perspective #2: Know that marriage is the union of two imperfect people

Rom 7:18 *For I know that in me (that is, in my flesh,) dwelleth no good thing: for to will is present with me; but [how] to perform that which is good I find not.*

You are weak, and you will make mistakes. God knows this and loves you despite your shortcomings; we call that grace. If God is gracious enough to understand this, then he is also able to teach us how to extend that grace to one another.

Perspective #3: Know that pride is at the center of all contention

Pro 13:10 *Only by pride cometh contention: but with the well advised [is] wisdom.*

It is pride that often sparks conflict and it certainly exacerbates it. Pride demands that "I am right, and you are wrong." Pride knows no bounds and has no limit to how far it can stoop. If in maturity we see our pride for what it is, then we will have the ability to die to our wants, desires, and "rights" and esteem our spouses better than ourselves.

Perspective #4: Address conflict before it escalates

Eph 4:26 *Be ye angry, and sin not: let not the sun go down upon your wrath: 27 Neither give place to the devil.*

If conflict goes ignored or neglected, it has the potential to turn into a root of bitterness or compound against other disagreements. Timely and patient communication can protect against the corrosive nature of unattended anger.

In marriage it is normal to disagree, but we must each avoid becoming disagreeable, which ultimately manifests in a destructive cycle of sin.

Perspective #5: Know that success or failure in marriage is a choice

Eph 4:29 *Let no corrupt communication proceed out of your mouth, but that which is good to the use of edifying, that it may minister grace unto the hearers.*

Even the smallest conflicts have the potential to disrupt unity within a marriage. This graph shows the two potential cycles that arise based on how you address conflict. You get to choose how to respond in moments of conflict and that response impacts whether or not you are promoting a cycle of unity or division.

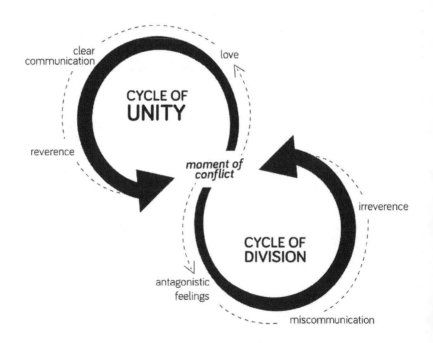

II. Principles for Problem-Solving

Problem-Solving Principle #1: Choose to walk in the Spirit

Gal 5:16 [This] I say then, Walk in the Spirit, and ye shall not fulfil the lust of the flesh.

Knowing God through prayer and abiding in his word daily produces a spirit-filled life and a holy lifestyle, or walk. If you are yielded to God, reconciliation and resolution become your desire.

Problem-Solving Principle #2: Open lines of communication prevent miscommunication

Pro 25:11 A word fitly spoken [is like] apples of gold in pictures of silver.

Transparency is an observable trait in strong marriages (Gen 2:25). Therefore, Christian couples should talk openly and honestly about their areas of weakness, areas of excitement, share their emotional expressions, personal vision, and personal concerns.

Problem-Solving Principle #3: Mature couples are able to address issues as they arise without hostility

Pro 15:1 A soft answer turneth away wrath: but grievous words stir up anger.

If you lead with love, respect, and a gentle response, then you invite the same speech in return. This is the beginning of healing and healthy communication.

Problem-Solving Principle #4: Unity is more important than being right or wrong, so take the wrong when possible

1Co 6:7 *Now therefore there is utterly a fault among you, because ye go to law one with another. Why do ye not rather take wrong? why do ye not rather [suffer yourselves to] be defrauded?*

This is a faithful declaration; God is bigger than your dispute! When we recognize this, it's easier to let go of our demands and expectations.

III. Principles for Engagement

Engagement Principle #1: Never engage in hard conversation when you are given over to your feelings

Pro 25:28 *He that [hath] no rule over his own spirit [is like] a city [that is] broken down, [and] without walls.*

If you try to resolve conflict while your feelings are not under the control of the Spirit, you are in danger of compounding the problem. It is wise to gather yourself and yield to God's word before you can earnestly work toward reconciliation.

Engagement Principle #2: Never assume you understand your spouse's thoughts and emotions without first listening

Pro 18:13 *He that answereth a matter before he heareth [it], it [is] folly and shame unto him.*

Jas 1:19 *Wherefore, my beloved brethren, let every man be swift to hear, slow to speak, slow to wrath:*

Don't function under personal assumption; take time to listen and consider your spouse's perspective without interjecting your bias. Listen with the intention of understanding, dying to self, and loving your spouse.

Engagement Principle #3: Never use destructive or hurtful language

Eph 4:29 *Let no corrupt communication proceed out of your mouth, but that which is good to the use of edifying, that it may minister grace unto the hearers.*

If you can't say something kind and constructive, remain silent. Claims of honesty and "rightness" are not an excuse to poison the conversation with name-calling or impulsive accusations.

Engagement Principle #4: Never devolve to physical conflict

Rom 12:10 *Be kindly affectioned one to another with brotherly love; in honour preferring one another;*

Arguments should never, ever get to this point. If you have a tendency to let your anger turn physical, then this is something that has to be given to the Lord and may require further biblical counseling. If one can determine to love someone more than themselves, then this issue will never arise.

Engagement Principle #5: Never go to bed with anger toward your spouse

Eph 4:26 *Be ye angry, and sin not: let not the sun go down upon your wrath: 27 Neither give place to the devil.*

God's instruction is that we deal with feelings of disdain toward our spouse before we lay our head on the pillow at night. This means either you work through reconciliation or you yield your feelings to the Lord so he can replace them with love and forgiveness before you close your day.

Engagement Principle #6: Always communicate that the objective is unity

Eph 4:1 *I therefore, the prisoner of the Lord, beseech you that ye walk worthy of the vocation wherewith ye are called, 2 With all lowliness and meekness, with longsuffering, forbearing one another in love; 3 Endeavouring to keep the unity of the Spirit in the bond of peace.*

Because God's objective is unity, we declare it as our objective as well.

Engagement Principle #7: Always remember that division is grievous to God

Pro 6:16 *These six things doth the LORD hate: yea, seven are an abomination unto him: 17 A proud look, a lying tongue, and hands that shed innocent blood, 18 An heart that deviseth wicked imaginations, feet that be swift in running to mischief, 19 A false witness that speaketh lies, and he that soweth discord among brethren.*

Because God hates division, we should do everything we can to fight against it.

Engagement Principle #8: Always be ready to forgive

Eph 4:32 *And be ye kind one to another, tenderhearted, forgiving one another, even as God for Christ's sake hath forgiven you.*

Be eager to forgive in order to bring things back to a place of unity. Because we are human and our hearts are deceptive, we may have to strive to forgive day after day in order to retain that unity.

Engagement Principle #9: Always be ready to confess your fault in the conflict

Jas 5:16 Confess [your] faults one to another, and pray one for another, that ye may be healed. The effectual fervent prayer of a righteous man availeth much.

Be eager to own and confess your faults and failures. Be ready to also own the perceived faults and failures.

Engagement Principle #10: Always protect the confidentiality of the conflict

Pro 11:13 A talebearer revealeth secrets: but he that is of a faithful spirit concealeth the matter.

Be careful not to share confidential information from arguments with friends, family, or people in church. Protect your spouse from judgment or hearsay by keeping the details of your conflicts between the two of you. In some cases, a couple may reach out to a counselor for help; in this case, the confidentiality must be shared in order to get proper help from a leader you trust.

Homework

The following are topics that most often cause conflict in newly married couples. Take time — not necessarily all in one sitting — to talk through each one of these to bring to light any significant differences that may cause trouble later.

- Address your philosophy of spending money which we discussed in the previous lesson. Is there anything that was missed that still needs to be addressed?

- Children — how many, how to raise, when can we afford them, does mom stay at home?

- The need for personal attention, making time to truly connect with each other. What steps will you take to avoid this common problem? Technology like TV, cell phones, or computer (over)use is commonly a big part of this problem.

- The need for alone time or time with friends. How often is acceptable?

- In-laws — do you foresee any problems in this area with your relatives? How will you establish and enforce clear boundaries?

- Traditions — what traditions are you bringing into your marriage? Things like, "But we always go to my grandmother's for Christmas." How do you establish new traditions as your family grows?

- Chores — who is going to do what chores in the new home? Plan now.

- As a husband or wife, have you reckoned the fact that you won't stay physically the same as you age? Is health important? Physical perfection?

- Do you tend to focus on being critical? How will you avoid bringing negativity into the marriage?

- What are your pet peeves? Anything that bothers you a little now may become a huge deal later. Does your future partner have any habits that annoy you? Be completely honest and talk through those things. Be willing to compromise.

If after discussing these you find that you have unresolved issues, let your counselors know ASAP so they can help. They likely have encountered similar issues in their past and can offer help based on their experience.

Lesson 5

Intimacy

The key word of this lesson:

CONNECTION

The key question this lesson answers:

How does a married couple establish and maintain connection in marriage?

The key purpose of this lesson:

To teach couples how to share intellectual, emotional, spiritual, and physical intimacy.

The key point of this lesson:

To reveal the importance of intimately pursuing your spouse and protect from growing distant.

The key verses:

Heb 13:4 *Marriage is honourable in all, and the bed undefiled: but whoremongers and adulterers God will judge.*

***1Co 7:3-5** Let the husband render unto the wife due benevolence: and likewise also the wife unto the husband. The wife hath not power of her own body, but the husband: and likewise also the husband hath not power of his own body, but the wife. Defraud ye not one the other, except it be with consent for a time, that ye may give yourselves to fasting and prayer; and come together again, that Satan tempt you not for your incontinency.*

I. Healthy Married Couples Pursue Intellectual Intimacy

When we describe intellectual intimacy, we mean connecting by sharing thoughts, ideas, and friendship in conversation.

Creating a Culture of Intellectual Intimacy

This means establishing a lifestyle of pursuing greater understanding in your marriage through communication.

- Do you make eye contact? Are you genuinely interested? **Mat 6:22,23; Act 3:1-8; Job 6:28**

- Do you put away distractions? **Pro 133:1; 1Co 7:35**

- Do you practice waiting your turn to speak? **Pro 18:13; 29:11; Jas 1:19-20**

- Do you listen carefully, noting the words of value? **Pro 25:11**

- Do you affirm? Are you gentle? Are you quick to forgive? **Pro 16:24; Eph 4:32**

- Do you complement each other in conversation? (Thoughtfulness, insight, maturity, etc.) **Eph 4:15**

- When you are confused, do you kindly summarize and ask them to confirm that you understand? **Pro 15:28**

- When you disagree, do you do so with gentleness? **Col 4:6**

- When conversations are inconclusive, do you point to prayer and patience? **Col 3:8; Pro 15:1**

- When you speak about God's will or what you are learning in the Bible, is it exclusive or inclusive? **Eph 4:15**

Safeguarding Intellectual Intimacy

- **Over time, communication in marriage can erode.** As seasons of life change, the lines of communication must adapt. If a married couple is not intentional about connecting intellectually, communication may devolve or grow cold and distant.

- **Be intentional about time together.** Ministry, friendships, and children are important, but should never keep you from making time one-on-one to simply talk or catch up on life.

- **Reserve your most intimate conversations for one another.** Family, friends, and co-workers should never substitute for the dialogue and relational connection between spouses.

- **Balance business and personal dialog.** Marriage is not a business arrangement, so make space in your conversation for all kinds of topics: everything from finances to friendship.

- **Protect against infighting.** When discussing emotionally charged topics such as major decisions or finances, always remember you are a team and you love one another — so guard your speech.

II. Healthy Married Couples Pursue Emotional Intimacy

When we describe emotional intimacy, we mean connecting by sharing our heart with our spouse.

Creating a Culture of Emotional Intimacy

This means establishing a lifestyle of empathy and support in all the emotional seasons of life.

Ecc 3:1 To every [thing there is] a season, and a time to every purpose under the heaven: ... 4 A time to weep, and a time to laugh; a time to mourn, and a time to dance; ... 8 A time to love, and a time to hate; a time of war, and a time of peace.

1Co 12:25 That there should be no schism in the body; but [that] the members should have the same care one for another. 26 And whether one member suffer, all the members suffer with it; or one member be honoured, all the members rejoice with it.

Php 2:4 Look not every man on his own things, but every man also on the things of others.

This might include:

- Happiness & Joy

- Sadness & Loss

- Anger & Frustration

- Disappointment & Failure
- Concern & Uncertainty

Safeguarding Emotional Intimacy

- **Focus your ears.** If you want to understand the emotions of your spouse, sometimes it's good to simply listen. We don't always need to provide an answer or an opinion, but rather respond with emotional support. We need to be careful not to assume the role of the Holy Spirit.

    Pro 10:19 In the multitude of words there wanteth not sin: but he that refraineth his lips [is] wise.

- **Protect yourselves from being controlled by your feelings.** We must not interpret our emotions in a way that leads us down a path of sinful thinking or activity. If our feelings become the authority, then Christ isn't. Feelings can be deceptive, so guard your heart.

    Pro 16:32 [He that is] slow to anger [is] better than the mighty; and he that ruleth his spirit than he that taketh a city.

- **In hard seasons, encourage your spouse in the Lord.** Sometimes feelings can be paralyzing or distracting from God's purposes. We must lovingly and patiently encourage one another to pursue faith in God's word.

    1Th 5:11 Wherefore comfort yourselves together, and edify one another, even as also ye do.

- **Be aware of what elicits emotional responses in your spouse.** The more you learn about your spouse, you begin to discover that certain things produce exceptional emotional responses. This might be memories, sensory experiences, or shifts in hormones. Being aware of these things will prepare you to have grace and love through those seasons.

Col 3:12 *Put on therefore, as the elect of God, holy and beloved, bowels of mercies, kindness, humbleness of mind, meekness, longsuffering; 13 Forbearing one another, and forgiving one another, if any man have a quarrel against any: even as Christ forgave you, so also [do] ye. 14 And above all these things [put on] charity, which is the bond of perfectness. 15 And let the peace of God rule in your hearts, to the which also ye are called in one body; and be ye thankful.*

- **Don't forget to celebrate in marriage.** As time passes, it's easy to let the business of marriage trade away your happiness for serious or stern feelings. Make space to joke around, play, and flirt. Find time to retreat together.

    Pro 17:19 *He loveth transgression that loveth strife: [and] he that exalteth his gate seeketh destruction.*

III. Healthy Married Couples Pursue Spiritual Intimacy

When we describe spiritual intimacy, we mean connecting by sharing our walk with God.

Creating a Culture of Spiritual Intimacy

This means establishing a lifestyle of worship and ministry together.

- **A husband and wife praise together.** A healthy marriage means practicing worship in one another's presence by professing God's goodness. This means you share words of adoration for God in conversation or in song.

Psa 150:6 *Let every thing that hath breath praise the LORD. Praise ye the LORD.*

- **A husband and wife pray together.** A healthy marriage includes praying together, conversing with God for every reason all the time. A seamless dialog with God within a marriage promotes reliance on God and openness within the family.

Eph 6:18 *Praying always with all prayer and supplication in the Spirit, and watching thereunto with all perseverance and supplication for all saints;*

- **A husband and wife ponder together.** A healthy marriage includes sharing what God has given you in the Word. These moments provide insight into how God is convicting and encouraging each of you day to day.

Pro 27:17 *Iron sharpeneth iron; so a man sharpeneth the countenance of his friend.*

- **A husband and wife partner together.** A healthy marriage is one where the couple shares in ministry opportunities. While each person might have distinct ministry responsibilities, at times there should be areas of overlap and cooperation in the mission.

2Co 6:1 *We then, [as] workers together [with him], beseech [you] also that ye receive not the grace of God in vain.*

Safeguarding Spiritual Intimacy

- **Maintain personal spiritual disciplines.** Each individual is responsible for their walk with the Lord. Whether in spiritual drought or abundance, we each own how we live life in relationship with Jesus Christ.

Psa 5:3 *My voice shalt thou hear in the morning, O LORD; in the morning will I direct [my prayer] unto thee, and will look up.*

- **Maintain joint spiritual disciplines.** This might look different for every married couple and does not need to be rigid or overly formalized. What is important is that you are intentional about finding ways of worshipping God daily and sharing his goodness. This is the purpose of marriage.

    Psa 34:3 *O magnify the LORD with me, and let us exalt his name together.*

- **Maintain a lifestyle of repentance.** A healthy marriage means that each individual deals with sin honestly as it arises in life and in marriage. This also means that we must protect ourselves from sin by refusing any and all provisions of the flesh.

    Rom 13:14 *But put ye on the Lord Jesus Christ, and make not provision for the flesh, to [fulfil] the lusts [thereof].*

- **Mold your marriage around the mission.** A purposeful marriage means that the couple is taking their cues from God's word, His Spirit, and the spiritual authority of the local church they are submitted to. God wants to use you, but a married couple must collectively determine that they want to be used.

    Act 1:8 *But ye shall receive power, after that the Holy Ghost is come upon you: and ye shall be witnesses unto me both in Jerusalem, and in all Judaea, and in Samaria,* *and unto the uttermost part of the earth.*

- **Make the local church an essential part of your family.** This means prioritizing the needs and purposes found in the relationships of our local church. A healthy married couple will faithfully attend, fellowship, give, and serve in their church.

    1Ti 3:15 But if I tarry long, that thou mayest know how thou oughtest to behave thyself in the house of God, which is the church of the living God, the pillar and ground of the truth.

IV. Healthy Married Couples Pursue Physical Intimacy

When we describe physical intimacy, we mean connecting by sharing in a romantic and sexual relationship.

Creating a Culture of Physical Intimacy

This means establishing a lifestyle that promotes a consistent and vibrant sexual relationship.

- **Sex with your spouse is a holy act.** This means that in the eyes of God, sex with the person you are married to is pure. Knowing that it is glorifying to God should give you liberty to pursue it without guilt or shame.

    Heb 13:4 Marriage is honourable in all, and the bed undefiled:

- **Sex with your spouse should be selfless.** This means that each spouse should be striving to please the other sexually. When both individuals reciprocate this sentiment, it produces shared pleasure and deep emotional connection.

***1Co 7:3** Let the husband render unto the wife due benevolence: and likewise also the wife unto the husband.*

- **Sex with your spouse should be enjoyable.** A healthy sexual relationship is uninhibited and exciting. When you come together this way, it should be a refreshing and invigorating experience — something to look forward to.

***Sng 8:14** Make haste, my beloved, and be thou like to a roe or to a young hart upon the mountains of spices.*

- **Sex with your spouse should be frequent.** A healthy sexual relationship means that a couple should be having sex as often as possible. There should be a culture of romantic anticipation and eagerness. A husband shows his love for his wife — no matter how busy or tired — by making himself available for intimacy any time that she desires. A wife reverences her husband by always conveying her permission to the husband in the bedroom, never saying to herself, "Why should I?" but rather, "Why not?".

***1Co 7:5** Defraud ye not one the other, except [it be] with consent for a time, that ye may give yourselves to fasting and prayer; and come together again, that Satan tempt you not for your incontinency.*

- **A proper approach to intellectual, emotional, and spiritual intimacy promotes a healthier and more consistent sexual relationship.** These other forms of intimacy have a unique way of culminating in physical intimacy. The way you encounter your spouse from day to day and moment to moment fosters a richer romantic connection.

Sng 8:7 *Many waters cannot quench love, neither can the floods drown it: if [a] man would give all the substance of his house for love, it would utterly be contemned.*

Safeguarding Spiritual Intimacy

- **Do not let sinful relationships from your past cause shame in your marriage relationship.** Many people have had sexual encounters in their past that were sinful. God is forgiving and gracious and wants to set you free from the shame associated with those experiences. Choose to trust God by turning over your thoughts and feelings, knowing that he has something very special for you in a romantic relationship with your spouse.

    Php 3:13 *Brethren, I count not myself to have apprehended: but [this] one thing [I do], forgetting those things which are behind, and reaching forth unto those things which are before,*

    Is there anything from your past that you have not yet shared in confidence with your fiancé/spouse?

- **Sex with your spouse is destroyed by pornographic thinking.** Pornography, sexually explicit entertainment, and romance novels are corrosive and dangerous to the health of your marriage. These indulgences are lustful and wicked, but also set false expectations for the bedroom. A pornographic approach to sex results in selfish behavior and a disappointing sexual relationship with your spouse.

    Tit 1:15 *Unto the pure all things [are] pure: but unto them that are defiled and unbelieving [is] nothing pure; but even their mind and conscience is defiled.*

Is there anything you need to speak to your counselors about concerning this subject?

- **Sex with your spouse should never be dishonoring.** If you are pressuring your spouse to do something they aren't comfortable with, then God is not in that.

1Th 4:6 That no [man] go beyond and defraud his brother in [any] matter: because that the Lord [is] the avenger of all such, as we also have forewarned you and testified.

- **Sex will grow cold and feel unnecessary if we aren't careful.** As time passes, it is easy to allow days, weeks, and months to pass between sexual encounters with your spouse. Unhealthy eating, lack of exercise, and general inattention to your body may compound the issue. It is important to remember that your body is not your own; it belongs to God and then to your spouse, so you should take care of it with the intent that you maintain sexual passions until the end of your marriage.

Abraham and Sara were intimate into their old age

Gen 21:2 For Sarah conceived, and bare Abraham a son in his old age, at the set time of which God had spoken to him.

- **Sex should never be a weapon.** When you withhold sex or use it as a reward to manipulate, then you are doing harm to the relationship.

1Co 7:4 The wife hath not power of her own body, but the husband: and likewise also the husband hath not power of his own body, but the wife.

V. Final Thoughts on Intimacy

The principles we have already provided about intimacy should give you a framework for a healthy sexual relationship, but we know sometimes newlyweds have questions of a much more practical nature. Even couples who have had sex before may find these basic tips helpful.

At this point in the lesson, we invite the couples to break out (girl with girl and guy with guy). This will give the conversation room to be more open.

Consider Your Approach

- **Initiation.** When you begin to engage one another, it is important that you consider your use of words. Are you inviting? Are you winsome? As the sexual encounter progresses, remember that prolonging your engagement helps heighten each other's sexual desires. This period of playfulness is often referred to as foreplay.

- **Be gentle.** The way you encounter one another physically is important. Don't be rushed and don't be rough. Take your time and be gentle. Maybe consider lubricant if necessary, particularly in the beginning.

- **Ask questions.** Talk to your spouse about what they want. This is especially important for the man. Listen to what your wife wants and put her desires first. For the wife, be clear in your communication and don't be afraid to guide him. This might feel awkward at first, but the more you communicate the easier and more comfortable it becomes.

- **Be patient.** This is a process of discovering one another, so don't be frustrated or discouraged if things don't go as you imagined in the early stages of your initial sexual encounters. Continue to talk and share, and eventually things will start to click.

Consider Your Hygiene

- **Be clean & groomed**. Make sure that your body is clean and smells good. Trim your fingernails and make sure your hands aren't rough. If you need to shave and take care of other aspects of physical preparation, then do so. Check your breath to make sure it's fresh; it's always good to have gum or mints nearby.

- **Use the restroom.** To avoid a urinary tract infection, visit the restroom shortly after having sex.

- **Clean up after yourself.** After you have sex you will want to clean up your body as well as the environment. Consider having towels nearby.

Frequently Asked Question:

- **What about menstrual cycles?**

    In these seasons, it is important to communicate and only engage sexually at the level you are comfortable with as a couple. Remember that variety is good, so consider trying other ways of pleasing your spouse. Again, be gracious and not insistent in moments that require sensitivity.

- **What about birth control?**

    Many young married women use a synthetic hormone birth control (i.e. pills, IUDs, implants). Others have personal convictions or physical reasons why they do not. In the case of those who do choose to use hormone birth control, it is important to know that there is a chance that it will produce varying levels of hormonal change. Consider starting several months before your wedding to see how it affects your body. For some women, the hormonal changes are excessive and not worth the physical stress, so they choose to use condoms or other forms of birth control (i.e. copper IUDs, diaphragms). Consider talking to your family physician or OB/GYN for more information.

- **What about sexual irregularities?**

    There are varying issues that some people may experience while having sex, including erectile dysfunction, soreness, or difficulty finding pleasure. Begin with prayer. Then consider asking personal health questions: is this related to my diet or exercise? Consider asking personal thought questions: is this related to the way I am thinking? If problems persist, meet with a physician to get their counsel.

In the midst of this conversation, make sure you leave space for question asking. If you have a specific question or something you are anxious about, this is your opportunity to get advice from your counselor.

After you have completed this lesson, the next time you meet you will already be married. In 3-4 four months and again in 5-6 months, you and your counseling couple will meet again to touch base and review how things are going. Schedule those meetings now.

If at any point between now and those scheduled meetings you have questions or needs, please feel free to reach out to your counselors. They are here to help you and guide you so that your marriage starts right.

Lesson 6

Moving Forward

Couple, now that you have been married for several months, you may be discovering that certain things have been easier and better than you imagined. You may also have discovered that certain things are harder. This is your opportunity to review some biblical principles with your counselors and ask new questions that you may not have previously considered.

Counselors, in advance of your meeting, develop a series of appropriate questions for the couple. Make sure that they address topics that you foresee being helpful to the couple. Reference the previously taught lessons to guide you in this conversation.

Examples may pertain to:

- How they are meeting their roles of marriage
- How they are integrating life and ministry involvement
- Their careers and financial situation
- Walking through conflict or their response to conflict

- Communication skills

- Aspects of intellectual, emotional, spiritual, and physical intimacy

After you have met in these two final meetings, counselors will remain available as guiding voices in your life. But if serious issues arise and you need further assistance in your marriage, they may defer to the assistance of a pastor in your local church.

It is so exciting to know that God has a perfect plan and purpose for our marriages. It is the hope of your counselors and those in your local church that your marriage will produce joy, fruitfulness, and blessing.

Made in the USA
Columbia, SC
21 June 2021